Inch by Inch

Elena Martin · Illustrated by Doina Paraschiv

Contents

Rigby®

A Harcourt Achieve Imprint

www.Rigby.com
1-800-531-5015

New Shoes

Rabbit needs
new shoes.

Will the red shoe fit?

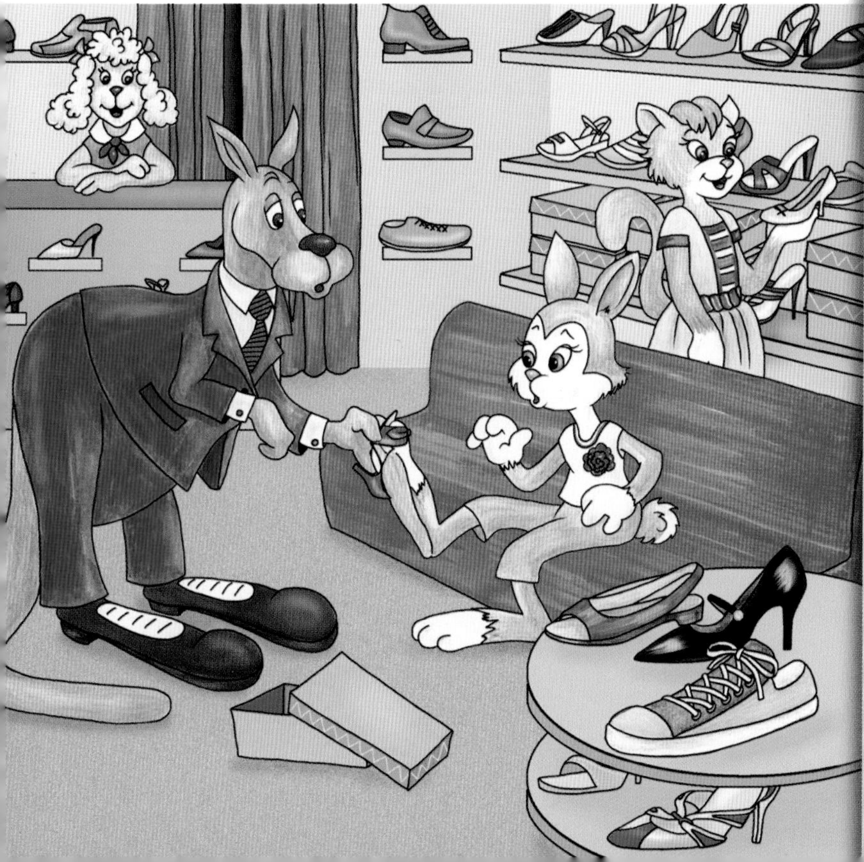

Rabbit needs new shoes.

Will the blue shoe fit?

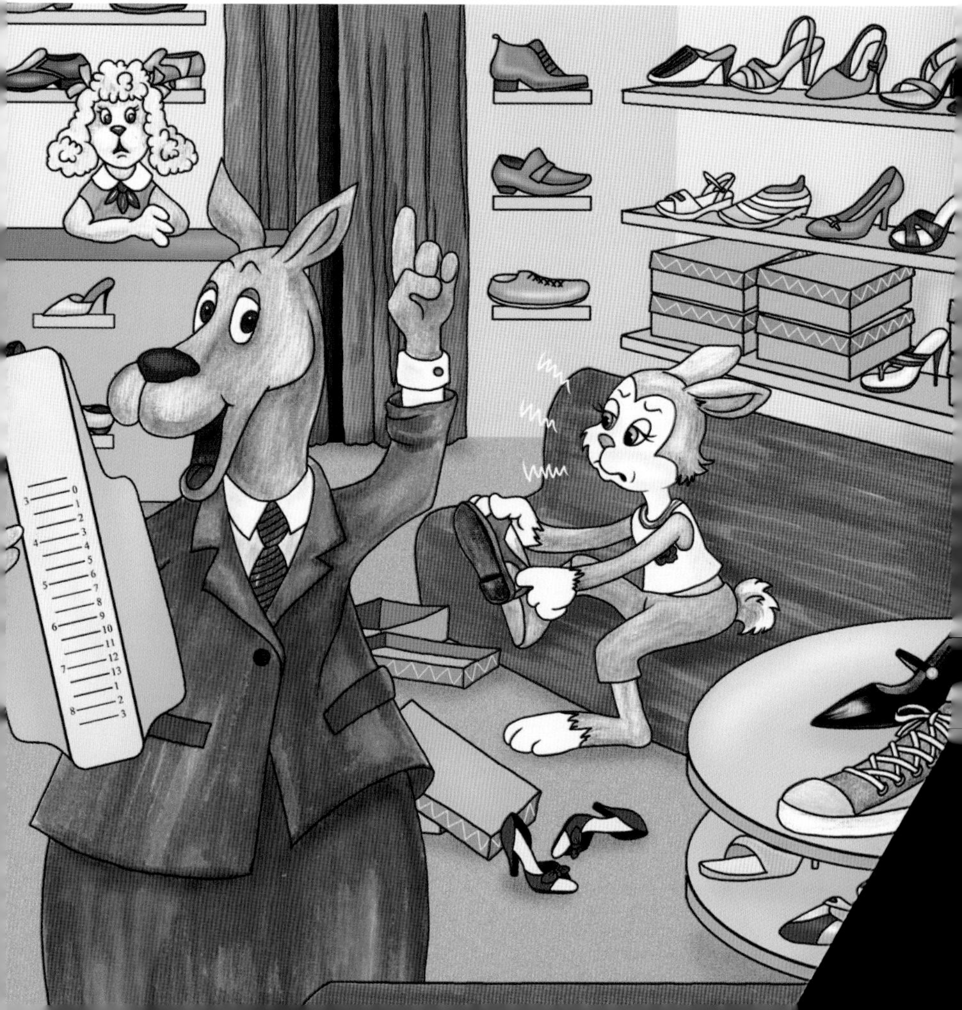

Rabbit needs

new   shoes.

Will the black shoe fit?

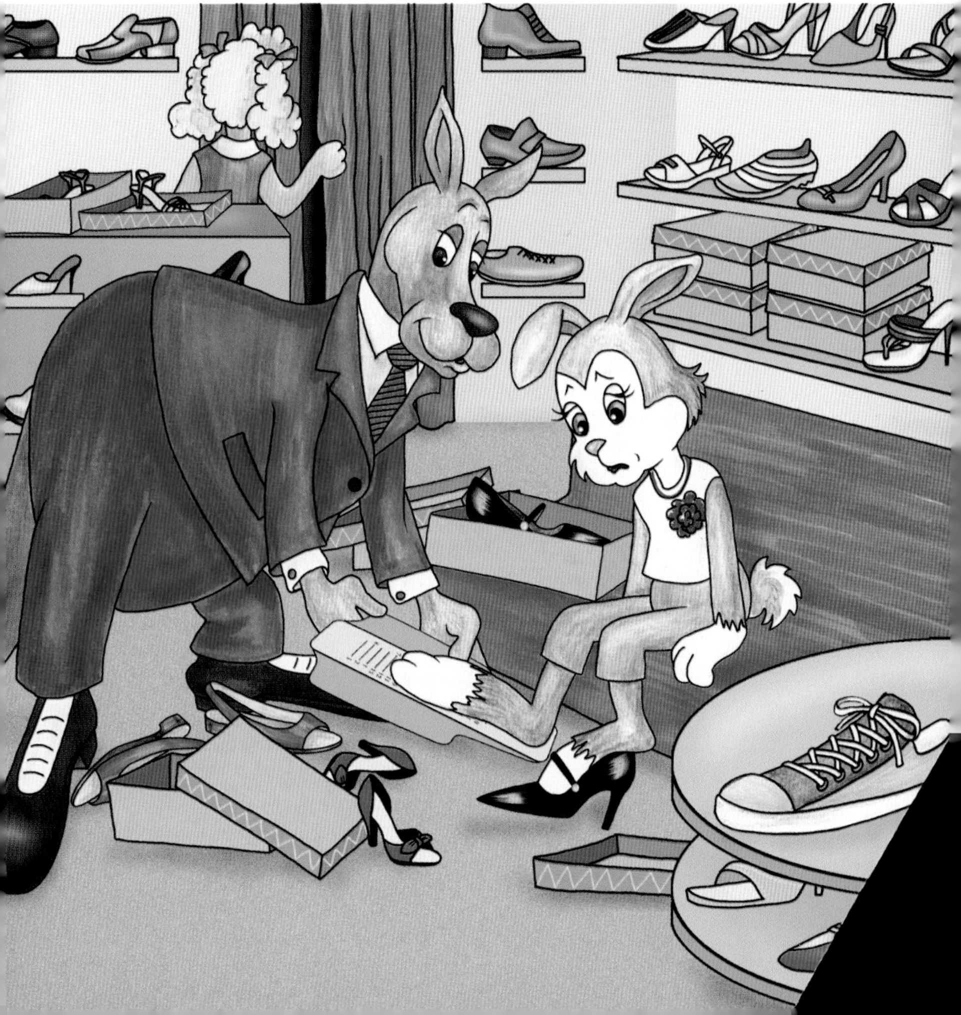

Rabbit needs new shoes.

The green shoe fits!

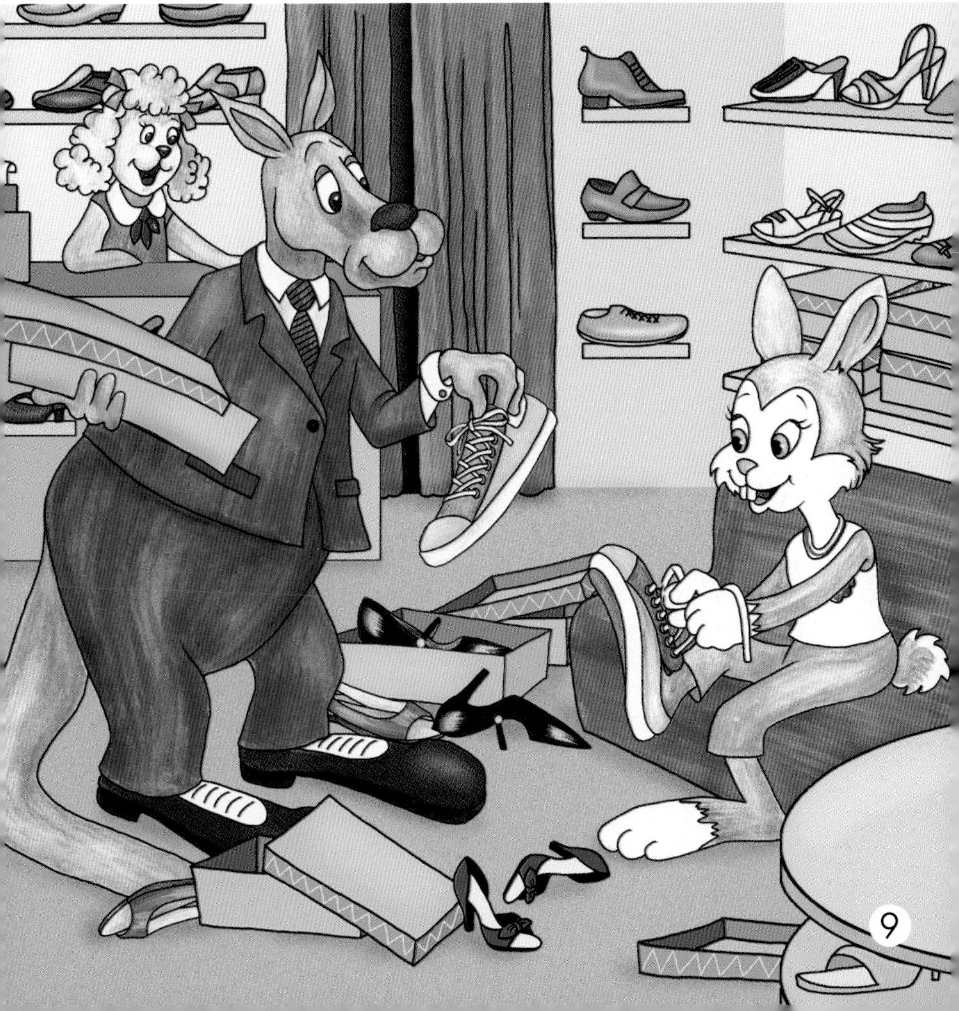

Measure It!

How long is this block?

Measure it!

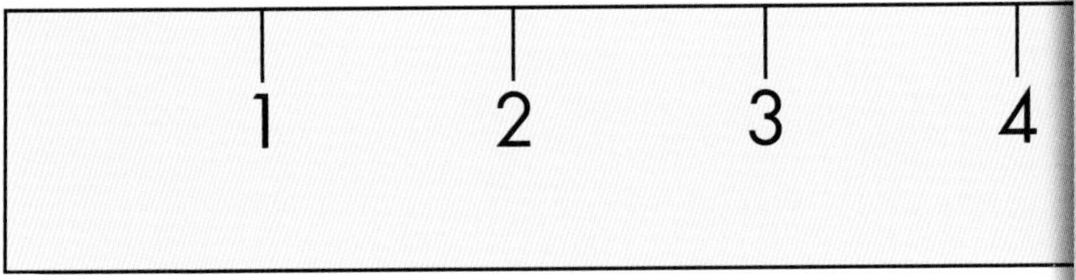

	1	2	3	4

How long is this paperclip?

Measure it!

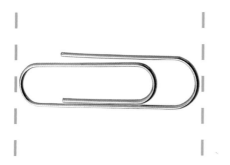

How long is this crayon?

Measure it!

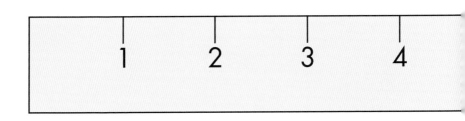

How long is this book? Measure it!